Contents

KT-572-621

① Introduction

Australia is an ancient land. It is so old that once-giant mountains have been turned into small undulating hills by the weather. There were once great and lush forests in the interior; they have withered into deserts.

Drifting continents

Australia was probably once connected to South America, but the continents separated as the Earth's plates moved. According to this theory, the land mass that we now know as Australia drifted into what became the Indian and Pacific oceans. It is thought that the marsupials we now identify with Australia, such as kangaroos and wallabies, were once animals that lived in trees, like the marsupials of South America. As the continents separated, and Australia dried out and the centre became a treeless desert, so the tree creatures learnt to live on the

Uluru

Uluru is one of the best known of Australia's many natural landmarks, and it is seen on many Australian postcards and in travel brochures. Uluru is also a place of tremendous cultural and spiritual significance for the Aborigines who live near it, and indeed, Aboriginal groups throughout Australia. For all Australians this largest of all known rock formations is the symbolic heart of the country.

PEOPLE UNDER THREAT

AUSTRALIAN ABORIGINES

Dr Richard Nile

First published in 1992 by Wayland
This paperback edition published
in 2010 by Wayland
Reprinted in 2010 by Wayland

Copyright © Wayland 1992
Revised and updated 2008

Wayland
338 Euston Road
London NW1 3BH

Wayland Australia
Level 17/207 Kent Street
Sydney NSW 2000

Series editor: Paul Mason
Designer: Kudos Editorial and Design Services

This edition
Wayland Commissioning Editor: Jennifer Sanderson
Design: Robert Walster
Editor: Sonya Newland

Acknowledgements
The artwork on page 6 was provided by Peter Bull and
that on page 23 was provided by Malcolm Walker. The
publishers would like to thank the following for allowing
their photographs to be reproduced in this book: Alamy
30, 38; Corbis 43; Mary Evans 10, 39; Eye Ubiquitous 4, 5,
7, 9, 11, 12, 13, 14, 15, 16, 16, 18, 19, 20, 21, 22, 24, 26, 27,
28, 29, 31, 33, 35, 36, 37, 40, 41, 42, 44, 45; Hutchison Photo
Library 32; Paul Kenward 8, 34; Zefa 25.

A CIP catalogue record for this book is available from
the British Library.

ISBN 978 0 7502 6373 3

Printed in Malaysia

Wayland is a division of Hachette Children's Books,
an Hachette UK company.
www.hachette.co.uk

This book has been produced in consultation with
the Minority Rights Group; an international non-
governmental organization working to secure justice
for ethnic, linguistic, religious and social minorities
worldwide who are suffering discrimination.

One of the Pitjanjara people of central Australia. He wears Western clothes, but follows the traditions and beliefs of his tribe.

ground. Nobody knows for certain how or when the Aborigines arrived in Australia. Nor does anybody know for sure where they came from. The oldest Aboriginal remains dated by modern scientists put the Aboriginal people at more than 60,000 years old. They have been in Australia for a very, very long time.

The Aborigines' own history tells them that they have lived there ever since Australia existed. Even if Australia was connected to South America or Asia, and even if the ancient Aborigines did travel across land bridges from other continents, then they were not travelling into new lands. They were travelling in parts of the same land, because Australia was not a separate place. Therefore, they were the first people of Australia, and not immigrants.

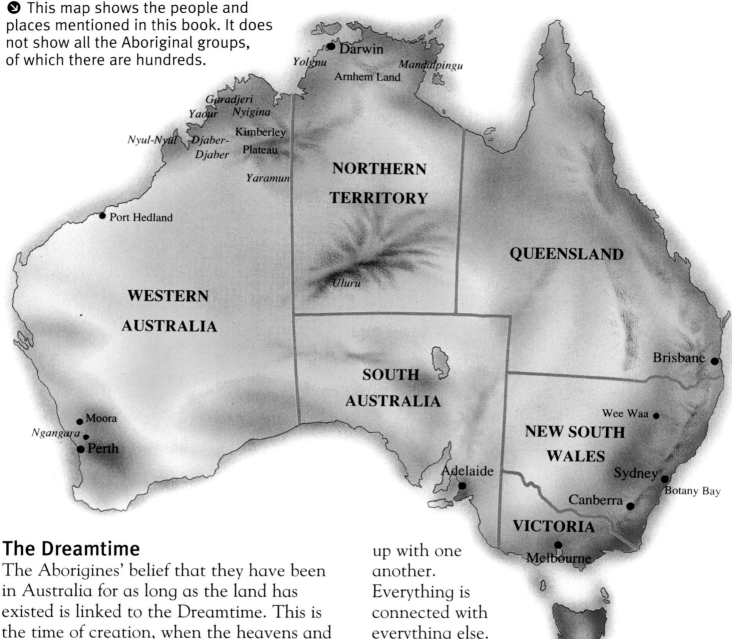

This map shows the people and places mentioned in this book. It does not show all the Aboriginal groups, of which there are hundreds.

Darwin

Yolngu

Mandalpingu

Arnhem Land

Garadjeri

Yaour

Nyigina

Nyul-Nyul

Djaber-Djaber

Kimberley Plateau

Yaramun

NORTHERN TERRITORY

Port Hedland

Uluru

WESTERN AUSTRALIA

QUEENSLAND

Brisbane

Moora

Ngangara

Perth

SOUTH AUSTRALIA

Adelaide

Wee Waa

NEW SOUTH WALES

Sydney

Botany Bay

Canberra

VICTORIA

Melbourne

The Dreamtime

The Aborigines' belief that they have been in Australia for as long as the land has existed is linked to the Dreamtime. This is the time of creation, when the heavens and Earth were one, and the ancestors were spirit men and women. The Dreamtime created heaven, Earth and the people as three different parts of the same thing, that should never be divided. All Aboriginal societies believed in Dreamtime, and because people were created from the land, they could not survive without it. According to Aboriginal myths, religions and beliefs, the land is the source of all life and meaning. The land and the lives of the people are intimately bound up with one another. Everything is connected with everything else. The land, the people, the flora and fauna were all created during the Dreamtime.

The Dreamtime is the single most powerful and important concept in the Aboriginal belief system. The Dreamtime exists beyond normal time and way beyond the collective memories, stories and knowledge of even the wisest elders. It is a sacred time; a time of great cosmic forces when the spiritual, physical and moral worlds were in the making. The whole Aboriginal universe dates itself back to this past.

The power of the Dreamtime

Aborigines believe that in death they will be reunited with their ancestors. They also believe that the Dreamtime will come again and give new life to traditional Aboriginal values and customs. This myth has been retold many times in terms of present-day dissatisfaction as a way of encouraging Aborigines to believe in a positive future. The Dreamtime is also a rallying political symbol, since it will result in a cleansing of the Earth and the return of lands to the Aborigines.

How the world was made

Aboriginal beliefs hold that in the Dreamtime, the ancestors came up from under the earth and walked over it, singing. What they sang was created as they walked. Their singing created the world, and they walked and sang until they were tired, and then they went 'back in'. The places where each ancestor went back under the earth are important religious sites, linked by the steps the ancestor took on his or her journey and the places he or she stopped to rest. These sites can be rocks, pools, hills and many other parts of the landscape.

⬆ This rock formation in northern Australia, the 'Devil's Marbles', has been deemed a place of evil spirits by the local Aborigines.

The Aborigines are a deeply religious people, but there are no priests in Aboriginal society, as there are in most other religious societies. Instead there are elders who translate the messages of the spirit world and pass these on to other tribal members. These men and women have special responsibilities and powers within Aboriginal communities. They are especially responsible for the young people in their communities.

Spirits of the earth

Traditional Aboriginal society is filled with rituals that relate to the spirit world. The spirits live in the earth and in the sky. They are everywhere and they give significance and meaning to the environment. A spirit can inhabit a desert flower, a tree or a bush; it can give shape to hills, plains and rocks; it can be seen at work in the habits of humans and animals. According to Aboriginal religion, the physical and spiritual worlds are one and the same thing. The earth is the mother of all things. If one is upset, the other will be as well.

Ritual and ceremony

Traditional Aboriginal societies have many ritual ceremonies. One of them is the *Corroborree*. A *Corroborree* is a ceremonial event that traditionally marks an important occasion in society. It is a festival of spirits.

◑ The didgeridoo is a traditional Aboriginal instrument, played at ceremonial events.

↑ These paintings at Kakadu National Park in the Nothern Territory are thousands of years old.

Corroborrees are normally held at night. They involve a lot of music, dancing and other rituals. Men and women are painted in sacred patterns with different coloured paints. These are made by grinding down rocks and mixing the powder with water, and oil from the emu. People also wear feathers and animal skins.

In traditional Aboriginal society, men and women have their own rituals, stories and ceremonies, as well as the ones like *Corroborrees* that they all attend. At a *Corroborree*, the men play didgeridoos, which are long, straight wind instruments made by hollowing out the branches of trees. The sound of the didgeridoo is haunting and quite unlike any other instrument. Its deep, growling noises combine with high squealing pitches. In dance, the men and the women recreate the characters of different animals. The men click their sticks, their boomerangs (special curved sticks) and their woomeras (spear-throwing tools) to keep the rhythm. People also sing when they are not dancing. Everyone sits in a large circle around the night-time fire.

Today traditional *Corroborrees* are held in secret for those initiated into the ways of ancient Aborigine customs. But comparatively few contemporary Aborigines know the ways of their ancient forebears, so they do not celebrate the *Corroborree* exactly as the ancient Aborigines did. But they do observe features of ancient ritual and many of the dances that have become popular art forms with contemporary Aborigines can be traced back to the old dances.

Bodysnatchers

During the nineteenth century, museums all over the world wanted to have the skeletons of different people from all different countries to keep in their collections, and they would pay a lot of money for them. Non-Aborigines, mostly Europeans, began stealing the corpses of dead Aborigines to sell their skeletons. When they could not find Aborigines who had already died they began murdering them.

Despite the fact that the skeletons were stolen and never had funeral ceremonies, many museums around the world still refuse to return them to their families.

Earth for all

Rituals, religion and Aboriginal customs are all means by which traditional society maintains links between past, present and future. Beliefs are passed down by word of mouth to each successive generation. *Corroborrees*, dance, music and stories all relate to the physical and moral world. This spiritual attachment to place also means that Aborigines do not believe in the concept of property. As nomadic peoples, they traditionally held that the abundance of the earth belonged to all that travelled on it. In present-day society they believe in equality and sharing. Just over 200 years ago, however, something changed the land and Aboriginal lifestyles forever.

The Europeans arrive

In 1788, the Europeans arrived with the intention of making permanent settlements in Australia. At first the Aborigines thought the newcomers were the spirits of ancient ancestors and that a new Dreamtime had begun. But the Aborigines quickly found out what the white settlers were really like. It was not long before the Aborigines became a group of people threatened with destruction.

When the first white settlers arrived in Australia in 1788, they immediately occupied Aboriginal land and began killing the fish and animals the Aborigines depended on. The Aborigines fought a guerrilla war against the whites, but were no match for the Europeans with their guns and horses.

The settlers could not understand that the Aborigines claimed land they did not physically occupy all the time as their own, and assumed that they could simply take it. When the Aborigines resisted, the settlers shot them. During the nineteenth and early twentieth centuries, many Aboriginal groups from coastal and eastern Australia were destroyed. The groups that survived were mostly those that lived in the interior.

Just over 200 years ago, the Aborigines made up 100 per cent of the population of Australia. Today they make up 2.4 per cent of the population. There may have been as many as three million Aborigines in 1788; nobody knows for certain. They now number about 400,000. Two hundred years ago there were more than 250 Aboriginal languages. Today, fewer than half that number survive.

2 Survival

Not far north of Ngangara, near the township of Moora, which is about 200 kilometres north of Perth, there used to be an Aboriginal reserve. It was closed down in the early 1980s but before that it had been the home of hundreds of people. Not far away, Benedictine monks and Methodist preachers had established missions, where they kept Aboriginal children who had been taken away from their parents. It was common practice then to take Aboriginal babies from their mothers and put them into institutions where they grew up without parents.

The Aboriginal reserve was located three kilometres out of Moora. The houses were not suitable for people to live in. Most were

⬅ These children live on the Mosman Mission. In the past, missionaries took children away from their parents and put them into institutions.

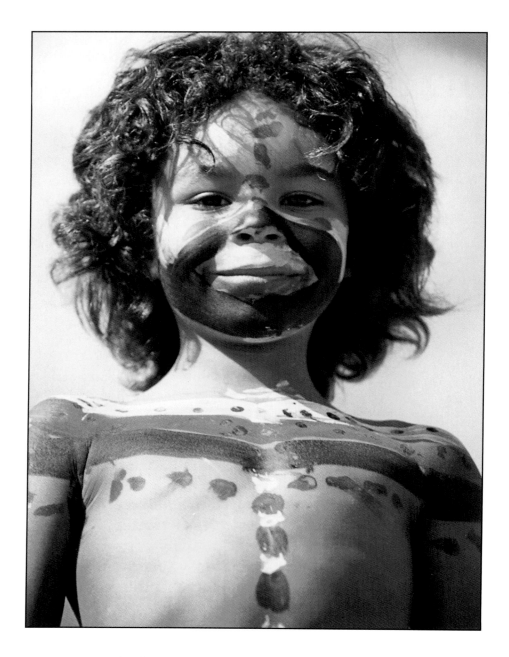

An Aboriginal boy with modern-style face and body painting. The design is a development from the face and body painting of traditional society.

one- or two-bedroom huts made out of corrugated iron. There was no insulation to keep out the great heat in summer or to keep the buildings warm in winter. There was no electricity or running water, and one toilet block served the needs of the entire makeshift community of 500 people, in which as many as five families shared a single hut.

Conditions on the reserves

The reserves created massive social problems throughout Australia, and the overcrowding and the insanitary conditions meant that infectious diseases soon spread. The children and the old people suffered most, especially in the winter. Colds and flu soon developed into pneumonia, from which many died. The houses were cold and the roofs leaked. Once the damp got into clothing and blankets, it was virtually impossible to dry them out. The clothes people wore, often given to them by charities, were no barrier against the cold and wet. The reserve system had to come to an end because it was so inhumane.

⬆ Aboriginal men in traditional face and body paint perform a traditional dance.

The last reserve was closed down in the early 1980s, but by this time a great deal of damage had been done. Given that the Aborigines were so badly treated in the past and that non-Aboriginal Australians have done their best to break down the structures of Aboriginal society, it is amazing that there are any Aborigines still living in Australia. Many of the traditional ways of the Aborigines may have been layered over by non-Aboriginal ways, but Aborigines are now proudly saying that they are both Aborigines and Australians. They are finding out more about their history and traditions. This is refreshing for many who were used to hearing themselves talked about in the terms that non-Aboriginal people used: hopeless, layabout or drunkard.

Paddy Roe

Paddy Roe was born in 1912 in the Nyigina tribe of the Kimberley region of Australia. Until his death in 2001 he kept tribal secrets for the Nyigina and for other tribes of the area, including the Garadjeri, Yaour, Nyul-Nyul and Djaber-Djaber. He called his homeland Gularbulu, which means the coast where the sun goes down. His tribal lands are made up of sandy beaches, undulating coastal foothills and mangrove swamps.

When he was a child, the police tried to take Paddy Roe away from his parents and place him in an institution, but he was saved when he was hidden away under a blanket while the authorities searched the campsite where his family lived. Each time the authorities came back he was hidden away.

Paddy became initiated as a full member of the Nyigina and later became the keeper of its tribal secrets. During his long life Paddy Roe was able to pass on to succeeding generations the secrets of his tribal history. If he had been captured and raised in an institution, these secrets would have been lost forever. The young people of the Nyigina are are fortunate to have learned about their past from this most renowned and respected elder.

Mixed-race children

Nearly 1,700 kilometres to the south of Nyigina territory is the city of Perth. There, Sally Morgan grew up in a mixed-race family.

⬅ This old man has a sharp bone, possibly taken from an emu, piercing his nose. Body marking is an important part of traditional Aboriginal life.

But she grew up not knowing her Aboriginal background. Her friends at school knew that she had dark skin but her mother told her that she was Indian. At school, Sally was treated as quaint, exotic and beautiful. Had it been known that she was an Aborigine, she would have been treated as inferior. Sally was always troubled by the story of her Indian past, and she could not understand why, whenever she had visitors, her grandmother would retreat into her room and refuse to be seen by anyone. Sally later learned that her grandmother was hiding the fact that she was an Aborigine. Sally could pass for an Indian at school and not many people seemed to identify her mother as an Aborigine, but her grandmother was obviously an Aborigine.

Sally eventually discovered that she was not an Indian whose parents had migrated to Australia but an Aborigine. At first she was shocked – surely she really was an Indian beauty, not one of those Aborigines? Sally's mother had spent much of her childhood in non-Aboriginal institutions; her grandmother had worked as a domestic servant for white cattle barons. Sally decided to find out more about her people and her own identity, which had been hidden away from her.

↑ An Aboriginal mother and her child. In the past, children from mixed-race marriages have hidden their Aboriginal background, or never been told about it, to avoid discrimination.

↥ This old photograph shows how traditional Aborigines used Western implements and adapted them to their own lifestyles – like the blankets covering the humpy (temporary home).

Redicovering a lost past

Sally's decision to find out about her background started her on a path that led to the discovery of a culture that would otherwise have been lost to her. She began by asking questions of her mother and grandmother. Eventually, she visited her grandmother's birthplace in the north of Australia. There she met relatives she did not know she had. She found out more and more about her own history and the history of her people.

Sally learned from her mother and grandmother about the cruelty that they had suffered at the hands of non-Aborigines. She came to understand that her family had hidden the fact that she was an Aborigine because she had a better chance at life in Australia if she was not thought of as an Aborigine. The decision was taken by the family so that Sally did not suffer in the way that her grandmother and mother had.

Telling the world

Discovering that she was an Aborigine and learning about her family's tragedies made Sally want to tell the world what had happened. She was determined to show everyone that she was an Aborigine, instead of hiding the fact. Sally Morgan's discovery of her true identity resulted in a moving book called My Place, which became a bestseller in Australia.

3 Past and present

In their own country Aborigines have been considered outsiders. They have been forced from many of their traditional lands, and not allowed to follow their traditional ways of life. Today, the Aborigines are fighting back and bit by bit they are beginning to win recognition of their civilization, so violently affected by the coming of the Europeans.

Sadly, changes have come too late for some people. The more positive and confident assertions of Aboriginal identity cannot help those who have died in police custody. They can only slowly begin to prevent the alcoholism and drug addiction that are so common in Aboriginal communities. They can only slowly improve

⬆ A way in which Aboriginal communities have sought to stop the devastation of their people by alcohol and drug abuse is to create alcohol-free areas called grog free zones.

◉ Friendships and political alliances cross racial boundaries.

the conditions under which most Aborigines live, and which most non-Aborigines accept as normal.

Australia's present-day population of more than 20 million is made up of people from many different societies, cultures and countries. They have all made new homes in Australia, which now hosts one of the most diverse collections of peoples anywhere in the world. The non-Aboriginal population, which can trace its origins back to Asia, Africa and the Americas, and most commonly Europe, lives side by side, mostly happily. The non-Aborigines are rightly proud of this achievement. Yet Australia's original inhabitants remain socially and culturally disadvantaged and subject to terrible racism. Where the non-Aborigines have tried to end racism among one another, they continue to practise it on the Aborigines.

Makarrata

The Yolgnu people of Arnhem Land have a special term that means the resolution of conflict. It is *Makarrata*. In traditional society *Makarrata* was usually reached only after lengthy discussions between the elders of the tribe. These discussions were held at *Corroborrees*. For the Yolgnu, *Makarrata* implies peaceful co-existence and harmony between peoples. Its meaning has now been expanded so that many Aborigines think about *Makarrata* in their dealings with non-Aboriginal Australians.

The Aborigines want to be able to negotiate with non-Aboriginal Australians on an equal footing, but many non-Aborigines remain suspicious of them. They say the Aborigines want to form a political structure like a parliament that has similar authority to the Australian parliament. They feel that such a body would mean that the

Aborigines want to separate from the rest of the country. But the Aborigines argue that for *Makarrata* to work, there must be full and equal discussion between both parties. They want an Aboriginal council through which they can negotiate with the immigrants to their country.

Land rights

The Aborigines have been forced by non-Aborigines to give up much that was once central to their society and culture. They have lost their lands, many of their languages and whole systems of belief. But they have not lost their identity as the first inhabitants of Australia. They now want to make sure that they are no longer treated as though they do not belong in their own country.

Most importantly, the Aborigines are calling for a *Makarrata* over questions of land. They want their claims to the land to be recognized by the non-Aboriginal law makers. Ultimately, this involves a fuller recognition of the Aborigine's rights to their own culture, which have been denied for so long. The land is sacred to the Aborigines of Australia and according to the Dreamtime myth, it is the source of all life. Even for contemporary Aborigines, living in the hearts of cities, the land is one continuous and massive place of worship. It is the spiritual base of the people. It is their home and the place of their well-being. Without

● The 1988 Bicentenary celebrations brought about both protests and friendships.

⬆ The Aborigines are not demanding the right to live in isolation, away from non-Aboriginal influence. They simply want the right to live as they choose.

the land the Aborigines feel they are separated from their life source, that they are separated from their spirit.

Today, Aborigines are claiming a right to the land, not only for religious reasons but also to allow their culture to once again flourish. With land, some would be able to continue their traditional hunting and gathering of food. Others could run their own cattle or livestock stations. But, in asking for land to be returned, the Aborigines are not asking for property rights in the way that non-Aboriginal Australian society understands property. For them the land cannot belong to an individual. The

Aborigines want to bring the culture and the land back into harmony and thereby reassert their Aboriginal identity.

Non-Aboriginal Australia has never formally acknowledged that the Aborigines are the original people of the land. In recent years Aborigines have begun to agitate to have part of their lands returned and to get some formal acknowledgement that the land is theirs – that the land was taken illegally. They want a treaty that gives full recognition of their claims. Such a treaty would also help other people to understand their claims for Aboriginal culture as a whole.

4 New Communities

One of the first things that visitors notice about modern Australia when they go there is how few people actually live in such a big place. Most Australians live in one of the six major cities, which are situated on the coast. Australia is about the same size as the United States (excluding Alaska), which has more than 13 times as many people. Australia is an island continent and the third largest country in the world. The distance between the east-coast city of Sydney and the west-coast city of Perth is the same as the distance between London and Moscow. Most of the country in between is desert and sparsely populated.

Another thing visitors notice about Australia is that there are very few Aborigines among the crowds who live in the cities. People of many different nationalities live there, but very few Aborigines. There are some Aboriginal communities in the cities, but the Europeans, who began settling in Australia 200 years ago, did not like having the Aborigines

⬆ The first settlement by non-Aborigines was made where Sydney now stands, and the Aborigines who lived there were forced to move.

there. As a result, most Aborigines tend to live on the fringes of cities and towns, or in outback communities. The other side of the coin is that in fact many Aborigines prefer to live in rural environments, as the land is very important to Aboriginal culture.

A case study

In the north-west of Western Australia, which is far removed from the cities, Tracey Nangala, an Aboriginal girl, lives with her family. She belongs to the Yaramun people of the Kimberley region, which is tropical on the coast and desert inland. She lives among her people in an all-Yaramun township. Tracey is taught the Yaramun ways and language but she also attends a school where she learns English, mathematics, social studies and all the things the non-Aborginal children of Australia learn in their schools.

On the other side of the Australian continent, Bunda Simms, who is around the same age as Tracey, attends the La Perouse primary school in Sydney and plays in the local junior rugby league team. Bunda speaks English with what is known as

◀ This girl is the product of two cultures. She shows all the outward signs of being influenced by non-Aboriginal culture but her identity is firmly Aboriginal.

These boys celebrate Aboriginal identity with distinctive T-shirts showing the Aboriginal flag.

the La Per Mob accent. Like Tracey, when he is at school he learns everything other children learn, but unlike Tracey he has not had the chance to learn any Aboriginal language.

Lifestyle differences

Many people would say that Tracey lives a life as close as possible to being a traditional Aborigine, while Bunda lives like the non-Aborigines. Certainly, they are both very different. Tracey's people still hunt and fish for their food, and they cook in ways that have been practised for thousands of years. She knows the stories of her tribal ancestors as they are told to her by the elders, and she will grow up knowing many of the secrets of her people.

Bunda, on the other hand, goes to the shops on Saturday mornings with his mum and dad to buy the family's food. He does not hunt and the only fishing he does is when he and a few friends ride their bikes down to Botany Bay – where white settlers

↑ Two hundred years ago the Aborigines could catch plenty of fish in Sydney Harbour, but now the water is too polluted.

first landed in 1788 – to toss their lines into the water. They do not catch many fish. The bay is so heavily polluted by large oil refineries and factories that not many fish survive in it. Bunda's family home is in the shadows of the large smoke stacks that now overlook Botany Bay.

A shared heritage

Tracey Nangala lives in the wide open spaces of the north of Australia; Bunda Simms lives in a cramped corner of the city. At first sight the two children of the case study seem to have little in common. Tracey would feel quite overwhelmed by the city of Sydney and

Bunda would get lost in the Yaramun country. However, they are similar in one very important respect. They are both descendants of the first people to live in Australia, and like their forebears, they have been treated unfairly and deprived of their rights and cultures by non-Aboriginal Australians.

The first people of Australia

Non-Aborigines sometimes make the mistake of saying that the only proper Aborigines today are those who live traditional lifestyles; that the only proper Aborigines are the 'full-bloods' and those who have not been influenced by non-

Aboriginal ways. Most of these people have been killed off or have died out since 1788. But if you ask the people from Yaramun country or from the La Per Mob, for example, they will state how proud they are of their Aboriginal heritage, and say they are true Aborigines. They believe that they are Aborigines by both descent and by inheritance.

When the Yaramun and the La Per Mob say they are Aborigines they are making a statement about their pasts and about their claims to be acknowledged as the first people of Australia. They are proud of their Aboriginal backgrounds, of their histories and cultures. No argument from non-Aboriginal points of view will make them want to be anything other than Aborigines.

⊖ This boy is wearing traditional face paint. Non-Aboriginal people often think that the only real Aborigines are those that look like this.

Ernie Dingo

Ernie Dingo is one of Australia's best-known actors and television personalities. He is a member of the Yamatji tribe, which inhabits the north-west of Western Australia. Ernie grew up in the town of Mullwela, where the local people still speak the traditional Wudjadi language. His birth name was Oondamooroo, which means 'shield' in this language.

Although he went to a non-Aboriginal school, Ernie was – and still is – proud of his background. After school, he spent some time as an Aboriginal culture officer, educating people in Aboriginal culture and heritage. When he became an actor and television star, he used his public profile to heighten mainstream awareness and understanding of Aboriginal history and traditions. Although he enjoys all the things that non-Aboriginal Australians do, he believes that Aboriginal culture should be respected and preserved. His presence on television and in films has made many people accept Aborigines as members of Australian society.

Traditional Aboriginal cultures

The mistake most often made by other people when talking about Aborigines is in their misuse of the word 'traditional'. When they say 'traditional Aboriginal cultures' they have in the back of their minds a world in which the Aboriginal way of life did not change for thousands of years. They are thinking of a world that stood still until the coming of the white people to Australia. What they have failed to appreciate is that Aboriginal culture has always been changing. Changes in Aboriginal civilization were not the same as those of other civilizations. As far as we know, Aborigines never developed a system of writing, for example. They probably remained hunters

⊙ These north-eastern Aboriginal women and men are celebrating their Aboriginal identity at an annual festival at Townsville, Queensland.

↑ This artist has painted a picture using traditional dot patterns. It is shows an atomic blast like the ones carried out by the British government at Maralinga in South Australia in the 1950s.

and gatherers rather than developing agriculture or fixed settlements. But Aboriginal society has developed and changed to fit the Australian environment. The direction and pace of change has altered since the coming of the non-Aborigines.

The Redfern Aborigines

In the middle of Sydney, not far from the central railway station and close to where Bunda and his family live, a settlement of Aborigines has taken over the slums and turned them into an Aboriginal suburb. Here, the Redfern Aborigines run their own housing authority, their own schools, radio station, theatre groups and their own legal service. To many Aborigines, the giant rock

Aboriginal art

To explain to children how parts of the land were made by different ancestors (see page 7), Aborigines in the central regions of Australia often drew maps in the sand. These showed where the ancestor started his or her journey, the footsteps they took while singing the landscape into existence, where they stopped to rest and where they returned to the earth.

From these sand drawings a style of Aboriginal art developed that has become world famous. Galleries in Sydney, London, New York, Berlin and Paris pay large sums of money for Aboriginal art. This money can be used to fund co-operatives and educational schemes in Aboriginal communities.

of Uluru (see page 4) in the centre of the continent is the spiritual heart of the country, while Redfern is the cultural and political heart of today's Aboriginal life. Redfern is the site where Aborigines have established their communities in defiance of intense pressure from some non-Aborigines not to do so. Redfern is a magnet for Aborigines from all over Australia.

The community began modestly in the 1930s, when Aboriginal workers and their families drifted into the city during the Depression in search of employment. Redfern was the cheapest and most run-down part of the city. It was also a convenient drop-off point for those arriving in the city because it was so close to the railway station. Above all, it was about the only place in the city, apart from the segregated area of La Perouse just to the south of Redfern, in which Aborigines could live during a period of terrible racial segregation in Australia.

In the 1970s, Redfern also began to attract middle-class and intellectual Aborigines, because it was one of the few Aboriginal communities in the city. Among those who came to Redfern in the 1970s were poets, artists and politicians. Soon after completing a Harvard PhD, Roberta Sykes moved to Redfern. She began campaigning for Aboriginal rights, including land rights and human rights. She met other influential people, including the Aboriginal magistrate Pat O'Shane and the actor Ernie Dingo.

⬆ Children learn about the richness of Aborginal culture. The performance takes place in the front of a massive backdrop of traditional Aboriginal symbols.

↑ A traditional sleeping shelter in northern Australia. Aborigines in Redfern have tried to make their houses have a similar 'open' feeling inside.

Strength in numbers

Roberta Sykes and her friends saw how the Aborigines could start to get other Australians to take account of their views. They saw the benefit of strength in numbers. Rather than choosing to move out of a poor part of the city as soon as they could, or simply never going there in the first place, they made their part of Sydney an exciting, interesting place for everyone who lived there. Soon, Redfern became the Australian centre of Aborigine cultural life. The radio station, the theatres, the schools and the legal centre all represent the success of Aboriginal culture all round Australia.

Redfern has improved the lives of the people who live there in many ways. Among the most important is the success of its housing policy. Redern had been the slum area of central Sydney for as long as Sydney had been able to call itself a city. It was characterized by rows and rows of messy terraces and semi-detached houses. But the Aborigines who live in Redern have adapted their housing to conform – within the confines of the city – with Aboriginal designs for dwelling. They call this 'indigenous inner-city architecture'.

Housing and community

The Aboriginal settlement of Redern from the 1970s onward happened at the same time as the city of Sydney itself began to change. Houses in old working-class areas were bought by wealthier people who liked the way they looked. The cost of housing increased so that many people could no longer afford to live there.

The Aborigines resisted this development, and instead began to change the housing in Redern to suit the needs of the Aborigines who lived there. The terraces remained in place but the inside walls were knocked down. Whole interiors were rebuilt to suit the needs of extended families, which remain the basis of Aboriginal society. The houses were completely different from buildings non-Aborigines lived in, which were meant for smaller families.

The terraces were also painted in the red and white ochre of the western desert, with splashes of other colours to reflect contemporary Aboriginal culture. The new colour schemes and murals replaced the grimy brick faces of the slums, which were transformed into places with an Aboriginal identity. At the same time, the narrow, enclosed verandas were turned into larger, communal areas. The few buildings that were knocked down made room for communal parks.

In Redern schools, which are run according to the needs of the community, Aboriginal children begin by being taught

⬆ Aboriginal students and parents demonstrate about the lack of Aboriginal studies taught in Australian schools. *Koori* is another word for Aborigine.

Australian band Yothu Yindi produces the annual Garma Festival of Traditional Music, celebrating Aboriginal music and culture.

Aboriginal languages, culture and history by Aboriginal teachers.

The residents of Redern today can listen to Aboriginal programmes on the radio that play music by Aboriginal performers, like the enormously popular Yothu Yindi, who incorporate traditional instruments and celebrate Aboriginal culture in their songs.

In Redfern there are also art studios and galleries featuring the work of Aboriginal artists such as Tracy Moffit. There are dance and theatre groups too, all owned and run by Aborigines.

Looking to the future

In Redfern today, traditional and modern Aboriginal cultures meet in a positive way. The past is remembered and treasured, but the community also looks to the future. Everything about Redfern – the terraces with their Aboriginal murals, designs and patterns, the legal service, the radio stations, the schools, the theatres, the art and recording studios – is a giant symbol of optimism. They tell the story of the survival of peoples who not long ago seemed likely to die out.

⑤ Police brutality

In many places across Australia, Aborigines have been treated brutally by the police. In an incident in 2004, an innocent Aboriginal man was killed while in police custody. He had been arrested on unwarranted charges of 'public nuisance'. While he was in the police cell, an officer beat him so badly that his liver was torn in two. The coroner concluded that the man had died as a direct result of the officer's beating, but the

⬆ A mass demonstration of 20,000 Aborigines, protesting against the high level of prejudice against Aborigines in Australia.

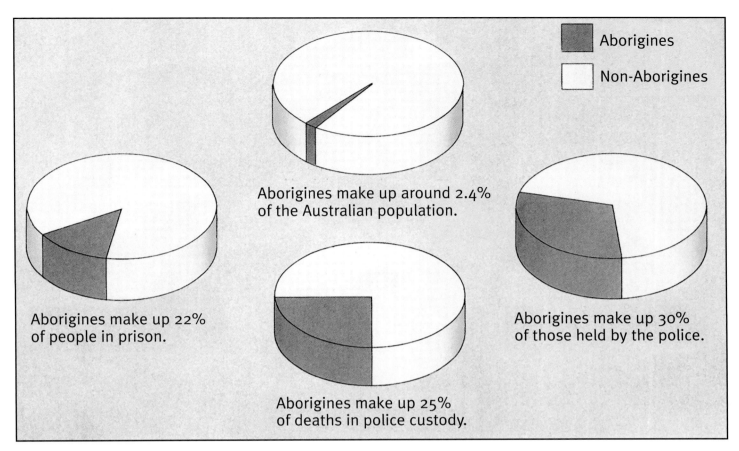

Aborigines make up around 2.4% of the Australian population.

Aborigines make up 22% of people in prison.

Aborigines make up 25% of deaths in police custody.

Aborigines make up 30% of those held by the police.

Aborigines

Non-Aborigines

⬆ These pie charts show that many Aborigines have had to deal with the police at some time.

policeman was not charged with murder. He was not even disciplined. The incident caused outrage. Many people demonstrated against this unfair judgement and called for someone to be held accountable for the man's death. But nothing was done.

Prison population

This incident was just one of many cases of Aboriginal people dying in prisons or while in police custody. Many more people die in detention than is commonly known. Although some inmates die naturally and others die as a result of accidents, some commit suicide or die violently by someone else's hand. Aboriginal deaths in custody are occurring at an alarmingly high rate in Australia.

Aborigines represent approximately 2.4 per cent of the population of Australia but they make up 22 per cent of the prison population. This means that if you are an Aborigine in Australia, you are 10 times more likely to be imprisoned than if you are a non-Aborigine. Aborigines also make up about 30 per cent of all people held in police detention, so if you are an Aborigine in Australia you are 20 times more likely than a non-Aboriginal person to be arrested and placed in the lock-up. Finally, although Aborigines make up only 2.4 per cent of the Australian population, they make up a quarter of all deaths in custody.

Very few Aborigines go through life without coming into direct contact with the police and courts. Most have experienced jail life or have friends or relatives who have been in jail at some time.

There are many explanations for the high rate of detention. Firstly there is the racism of the police forces, who for many years have

⊕ Police are being trained not to discriminate against Aborigines, but there is still a long way to go before prejudice is broken down.

discriminated against Aborigines without having to answer for it to any higher authority. For the police, the Aborigines have been easy pickings. The courts may not have been as biased against Aborigines as the police, but they have generally believed the police's version of events. This has happened even in cases where independent witnesses have testified against methods of arrest, and where police have used excessive force. More than one court has heard witnesses tell how innocent Aborigines have been wrongly arrested, but until recently this has made little difference and Aborigines have been wrongly convicted.

In many areas Aborigines have either inadequate legal representation or none at all. When they do have proper legal help, the conviction rate drops. The Aboriginal Legal Service, in which Aboriginal and non-Aboriginal lawyers work together, is helping to make sure that increasing numbers of Aborigines are legally represented.

The problem is made worse by the generally low social and economic position that the Aborigines occupy in Australia. Despite the successes of Redfern and similar communites elsewhere in Australia, many Aborigines live in a more or less constant state of poverty and homelessness. Some of them can provide themselves only with a reasonable standard of living by stealing. They also come into conflict with non-

Aborigines whose standard of living is much higher than their own.

Reasons for high crime rates

Some Aborigines see crime as a means of relieving boredom. Among teenagers in particular, where younger teenagers stay away from school and older teenagers are often unemployed, joy-riding in stolen cars has become a dangerous way of finding something different to do. Alcohol and drug taking are also reactions to poverty, and are closely linked to crime. Alcohol and drugs make a lethal cocktail in a stolen car, and many people have been killed and injured.

When non-Aboriginal people have been killed in the recklessness, anger against Aborigines has intensified. In 1992, in

⬆ The poverty in which many Aborigines live has been blamed for the high Aboriginal crime rates.

Western Australia, very harsh penalties were introduced to try to stop joy-riding. Imposing punishments did not help, though, because they did not address the causes of the problem – the poverty in which many Aborigines lived, and the low social position they felt they held in society. It is hard to see how long prison sentences help.

The death of Eddie Murray

In recent years, Aborigines have died in custody in Australia at the rate of one every two weeks. A national inquiry into Aboriginal deaths in custody found three main causes of death: suicide, violence and natural causes. Among the most famous cases was that of Eddie Murray. Aged 21 when he died, Eddie Murray was from Wee Waa in New South Wales. He was arrested for drunkenness, and later found hanged in his police cell. At the time, Eddie, who had been a champion footballer, was the only prisoner in the cell. His cell had been locked with a key that only the police had access to. The coroner found that he had been killed 'at the hands of a person or people

⬆ Aboriginal demonstrators protesting against the rate of detention of Aborigines in Australian prisons.

⬆ Despite a commission of inquiry that handed down its judgement in 1991, people are still angry and afraid about Aboriginal deaths in custody.

unknown'. To this day, nobody has been arrested for his murder. Many police forces in Australia have recorded similar cases of suspicious deaths in custody.

The death of John Pat

A commission of inquiry was begun after the death of a 16-year-old, John Pat, who died in his prison cell after being arrested in Port Hedland in Western Australia. Several people saw five policemen repeatedly kick John Pat after he had been knocked to the ground during a disturbance. He died of a brain haemorrhage in his police cell a few

hours later. The police officers denied that they had kicked John Pat and claimed that they had used no more force than they normally would while arresting someone. A separate investigation was held, but no one was ever charged.

Prison suicides

The commission of inquiry, which handed down its findings in 1991, noted that suicide rates were high among Aboriginal prisoners. Many hanged themselves using shoe laces, football socks, belts or blankets. The reason for the high occurrence of suicide is not known.

At Redfern these protesters draw attention to the killing of an innocent man, who was asleep in his bed when the police broke into the house and shot him.

Alcohol and drugs are sometimes blamed, especially when they lead to depression or hallucinations. A commonly held theory is that, terrified by isolation and confined areas, Aborigines under the influence of drugs or alcohol believe they are being possessed by evil spirits. But more generally, for people so used to wide open spaces, confinement is horrific.

Most people agree that too many Aborigines end up in Australian jails and that strong action should be taken to stop the deaths in custody. Programmes aimed at breaking down police prejudices have been in force for some years. Efforts are also being made to recruit Aboriginal police officers to try and establish an equality in the police force. Despite this – as video evidence of police violence against an Aboriginal man in a 2001 court case proved – many parts of the country are slow to change their attitude, and police brutality continues.

6 Education

Australia has one of the highest standards of living in the world. It is a society where most people would claim that there are equal opportunities for everyone. But of all the ethnic groups that live in Australia, the Aborigines are socially and culturally the most disadvantaged. They occupy the lowest position in just about every aspect of society as measured by health, living conditions, education and employment. They live, on average, 20 years less than non-Aboriginal Australians. Infant mortality is shockingly high in comparison with non-Aboriginal groups. The conditions under

↑ Demonstrators draw attention to the low life-expectancy and shocking level of infant mortality among Aborigines.

which the majority of Aborigines live resemble in many ways those of the world's poorest countries, rather than those of one of the world's richest. Part of the reason for this is the years of neglect by non-Aboriginal policy makers. Apart from training Aborigines to a low level where they could read and write (though many are still illiterate), until quite recently teachers were not trained to cope with the special needs of Aboriginal children. Most teachers seemed to be quite uninterested in passing on to Aborigines the benefits of a good education. As a result of their own efforts, and with some help from the government, opportunities for Aborigines to become doctors, lawyers and headteachers have increased. But Aboriginal children are still likely to leave school at an early age, and comparatively few make it into universities or other institutions of higher education.

⬆ These Aboriginal children attend school on the Tiwi Islands, in Australia's Northern Territory. There, more than 90 per cent of the population is Aboriginal.

⬆ In remote outback areas, children may not learn English until they go to school. This puts them at a great disadvantage in all their classes, which are taught in English.

Special needs

Recently teachers have looked into the ways the Australian education system has treated Aboriginal children, and most agree that the ways schools are run in Australia have not addressed the special needs of Aboriginal students. One of the key problems is that for many Aborigines, English is a second language, but it is taught in schools as a first language. So when teachers speak to Aboriginal students they do not take account of the fact that many are used to speaking a different language. This language problem is most obvious in areas in the outback where traditional languages are still spoken. But even in the cities and the towns where many of the old ways have been lost, the Aborigines speak Creole. This is a combination of English and the Aboriginal language.

The fact that many Aboriginal children are more familiar with their traditional language than English has only recently been taken into account. Aborigines are no

① Some attempt has been made at this school at the Stirling Station to make the heat bearable. Still, the children prefer to be taught outside where it is cooler.

more or less intelligent than their non-Aboriginal counterparts. The two peoples simply look at things in different ways and think about these things using different languages. The school system favours English, so not surprisingly, the Aboriginal children tend to fall behind.

Status in schools

Most Aboriginal children have been educated under this system and have suffered as a consequence. As they become identified as having learning difficulties, any hopes they might once have had of success at school disappears. Teachers begin to expect Aborigines to fail, and Aboriginal students are put at the bottom of the class before the first tests are taken. This means that even those who have good English language skills and who are capable of advancing under the system, suffer unfairly. There is very little in the Australian education system for Aborigines. It merely confirms their low status in society and reinforces in non-Aboriginal people the view that Aborigines are inferior.

Forces of change

Educators are now trying to improve the situation, but they have to try and change the practices and perceptions of more than 200 years. It is likely to take several generations of teachers and students, both Aboriginal and otherwise, to change the situation. But the change has started and special language training for teachers and Aboriginal students has begun. There are now a few schools that specialize in Aboriginal languages. At these schools English is taught as a second language.

Aboriginal schools

In Western Australia, Aboriginal elder Ken Colbung started an all-Aboriginal school called Ngangara. Here, the students learnt first about their own customs and cultures and then applied what they learnt to their other subjects. The school proved a great success and Aboriginal children left it with a better chance of succeeding in the outside world than other Aborigines who attended non-specialist schools.

The Aboriginal students who are now graduating from specialist schools are no different in terms of their academic achievements from non-Abriginal children. There is a lot of pressure on these students to succeed educationally and return to the school system, where they will take on the responsibilities of teaching a new generation of Aboriginal students.

Aboriginal rights campaigner Paul Coe speaks out about racism in Australian schools.

7 The future

On Australia Day, 26 January 1988, non-Aboriginal Australia was in a mood for a party. The day marked 200 years since the first white people had come to live in Australia. Out of very little these people had built one of the most successful societies in the world. Their forebears had overcome some of the most difficult territory in the world and come together over enormous distances to form a single nation. All around, people could see what had been accomplished over two centuries.

On the very same day the largest gathering of Aborigines since the Dreamtime took place at the site where the white celebrations were happening. More than 20,000 Aborigines from all parts of Australia assembled first at Redfern and then marched down to Sydney Harbour. Theirs was not a day of celebration but a day of remembrance, on which all Aborigines commemorated their ancestors and reminded non-Aboriginal Australians that their achievements had come at a cost of massive suffering.

⬆ The centenary celebration marches past the centenary demonstration.

⬆ The Aboriginal demonstration on Australia Day ends on La Perouse beach, where white explorers first landed 200 years before.

Two tribes

The two tribes of Australia – the Aborigines and the non-Aborigines – came face to face with one another. Their two *Corroborees* became a single event. Although the non-Aborigines had set out to celebrate the achievements of their pioneers, many finished the day thinking more and more about the Aborigines. Something very important happened on Australia Day: a new beginning was made. It was the start of a period in which the Aborigines started to be recognized as an integral part of Australian society.

On the other side of the globe, a smaller but no less important event happened. Aboriginal elder Burnum Burnum, from the Aboriginal peoples of Eastern Australia, planted an Aboriginal flag at Dover, England and claimed the whole of the United Kingdom on behalf of the Aboriginal peoples of Australia. The protest, of course, was symbolic.

Hopes for the future

Twenty years after the Bicentenary, the picture of the Aborigines of Australia is still a mixture of dismay and hope. On the one hand Aboriginal culture is in crisis. Many communities are characterized by alcoholism, drug taking, and violence. But some are now claiming better education and housing, and insisting on being treated equally. For them the future is an exciting place where Aborigines and non-Aborigines stand as equals; where Aboriginal culture is thought to be important to all Australians.

Glossary

Aborigine The first occupants of any land. Often used more specifically to mean the 500 or so tribal groups of pre-colonization Australia. The words *Nyoongar* and *Koori* are also used to describe them.

Cattle barons Owners of large areas of land on which huge herds of cattle are raised.

Corroborree An Aboriginal celebration, including music and dancing.

Depression The name of a time in the early 1930s when very few people had jobs or enough money to live on.

Dreamtime An English term used by Aborigines to refer to the time of creation.

Emu Large birds that live in Australia. They cannot fly, but run quickly.

Full-blood An English term for Aborigines whose families have never had children with white people and who have not adopted many non-Aborigine ways.

Guerilla war A war in which one side tries to stay hidden from the other, attacking in unexpected places and disappearing before they are caught.

Infant mortality The number of babies in every thousand born that dies. Infant mortality is used to measure how good health care is in particular groups of people.

Joy-riding Driving very fast in a stolen car.

Marsupial Mammals whose young are born and then continue to develop in a 'pouch'.

Mission Places at which representatives of one of the Christian religions live. They try to make the local people join their religion.

Nomadic Constantly moving, usually in search of food and pasture for animals.

Ochre Orange or yellowish-orange.

Outback The remote, wild country away from the settled areas of Australia.

Polluted Made unclean or not pure.

Prejudice An idea of what someone or something will be like before you have met or seen them. For example, if you thought all Aborigines were stupid but had never met one, you would be prejudiced against Aborigines.

Racist Prejudiced against someone because of their race.

Reserve An area of land set aside for the use of a particular group of Aborigines.

Rural In the countryside; away from the towns and cities.

Segregation Keeping things apart. Most often used to describe the policy of racial segregation; making people with different-coloured skins live in different areas. See Apartheid.

Suburb An area in which people live outside the centre of a city.

Uluru The enormous rock in the desert at the centre of Australia, which has great spiritual significance for the Aborigines. It is also called Ayers Rock.

Urban Part of the city.

Woomera An implement used to throw a spear.

Further reading

Gularbulu Paddy Roe (Fremantle Arts Centre Press, 1983)

The Songlines Bruce Chatwin (Picador, 1988)

Uluru: Australia's Aboriginal Heart, Caroline and Arthur Arnold (Clarion Books, 2004)

Indigenous Peoples: Aboriginal Australians, Diana Marshall (Weigl Publishers, 2003)

The Aboriginal Peoples of Australia, Anne Bartlett (Lerner Publishing, 2001)

Aboriginal Art and Culture, Jane Bingham (Raintree, 2005)

Further Information

Australian High Commissions and Embassies in your own country are a good first stop in your search for more information. You could also try the following:

Australia

The Aboriginal Centre
Old Clontarf Boys Home
Manning Road
Waterford 6152

Australian Institute of Aboriginal Studies
PO Box 553
Canberra 6152

Redfern Legal Centre
Everleigh Street
Redfern 2016

Canada

Indigenous Survival International
47 Clarence Street
Suite 300
Ottawa
Ontario K1N 9K1

UK

Mr James Hunt AO
Australian Book Shop
10 Woburn Walk
London WC1

Minority Rights Group
379 Brixton Road
London SW9 7DE

USA

Survival International
2121 Decataur Place NW
Washington DC 20008

Index

Numbers in bold refer to pictures as well as text